T0110881

Spiritual Deception

"Be not deceived, God is not mocked,
for whatever a man soweth, that shall
he also reap" Galatians 6:7, KJV

Dr. Larry E Adams

WESTBOW
PRESS®
A DIVISION OF THOMAS NELSON
& ZONDERVAN

WestBow Press books may be ordered through booksellers or by contacting:

WestBow Press
A Division of Thomas Nelson & Zondervan
1663 Liberty Drive
Bloomington, IN 47403
www.westbowpress.com
844-714-3454

Scripture taken from the King James Version of the Bible.

ISBN: 978-1-6642-1032-5 (sc)
ISBN: 978-1-6642-1031-8 (e)

Print information available on the last page.

WestBow Press rev. date: 04/16/2021

Why boastest thou in thyself in mischief O mighty man? The goodness of God endureth continually. Thy tongue deviseth mischiefs, like a sharp razor, working deceitfully. Thou lovest evil more than good, and lying rather than to speak righteousness. Thou lovest all devouring words, O thou deceitful tongue. Selah. God shall likewise destroy thee forever; he shall take thee away, and pluck thee out of thy dwelling place, and root thee out of the land of the living. Selah. The righteous also shall see and fear, and shall laugh at him: Lo, this is the man who made not God his strength, but trusted in the abundance of his riches, and strengthened himself in his wickedness.

Psalms 52: l-7, KJV

DEDICATION

I write this book to the Church of Jesus Christ. All those whose doors stand ajar in His name and for the love of the Spirit of God. Realizing that He is worthy of all possible honor, confidence and love to the glory of God the Father. We give Him praise and hope that this book will change lives in the name of our Lord and Savior Jesus Christ.

CONTENTS

FOREWORD

"Beware lest any man spoil you through philosophy and vain deceit, after the tradition of men, after the rudiments of the world, and not after Christ." (Colossians 2:8, KJV) Though a warning by Paul to the Colossians it was not understood what had been revealed to them of the things that would come upon them as believers and members of the body of Christ. The error against which Paul warned the Colossians later developed into the heresy called Gnosticism. They were about to be deceived into false mysticism and asceticism. (Colossians 2:18-23, KJV) Spiritual deception is *spiritual* and is the number one tool of Satan the great deceiver and father of lies. (John 8:44, KJV) We are living in the age of deception and according

to Genesis 3:4 deception will only increase through time, some shall depart from the faith giving heed to seducing spirits, and doctrines of demons speaking lies in hypocrisy, having their conscience seared with a hot iron." (I Timothy 4:1-3, KJV)

Now that we know that spiritual deception is a ruse, a device used to mislead or confuse, to avoid this deception we must abide in the word of God. Logics and intelligence will not protect us from spiritual deception. The power of deception comes when we turn away from the truth or to make something that is false appear to be true. This deception can come from ourselves, other people and from deceiving spirits. We know that spiritual deception is a powerful issue and we hope to reveal how it effects our living, our worship and our understanding of Gods purpose for our lives. We have been warned by the truth of Gods word and made aware of the enemy that we should prepare ourselves realizing that we are never alone but have the responsibility to trust God who sees all and knows all.

INTRODUCTION

Deception is spiritual because it originated from Satan who is a created spiritual being. According to the Bible God created Satan as: *"the anointed cherub that covereth, and I have set thee so; thou wast upon the holy mountain of God; thou hast walked up and down in the midst of the stones of fire. Thou wast perfect in thy ways from the day that thou wast created, till iniquity was found in thee". (Ezekiel 28:14-15, KJV)* From this statement of God we know without a doubt that deception is a sin. (Ezekiel 28:16, KJV) As the result of this Lucifer was casted out of heaven to the earth. Ever since Eve was deceived in the Garden of Eden that led to the voluntary transgression of Adam, the nature of man became sinful. (Isaiah 14:13-14, KJV) It is amazing even in these times how the creature will put himself above the creator. Nevertheless that same deception of lies and imagination followed Satan to the earth as he became the great deceiver. (I Peter 5:8, KJV) (Revelation 12:9,13:14, KJV)

Ever since the fall of Satan he has attacked the minds of men through imaginations and deceits turning the truth into unrighteousness. (Romans 1:18,25, KJV) We may not be aware that an imagination is the introduction to a lie and is not backed by truth. That's why it's called an imagination. Deception has become a part of man's way of life good or bad especially in compromising God's word. The Lord gave us a covenant not a compromise. Scripture teaches that there is a way that seemeth right to a man but the end is the way of death. (Proverbs 14:12, KJV) So why do people imagine a vain thing? A purpose that will come to nothing? Because they have been deceived. (Psalms 2;1, KJV) Most people don't realize that deception is as much spiritual as it is physical. We mislead others many times through lies, persuasions, compromising and deceit physically but because of the spirit that you have leads you to that point. (Romans 7:18-23, KJV) God has warned us to be aware of our responsibility; *"be not conformed to this world, but be ye transformed by the renewing of your mind, that ye may prove what is that good, and acceptable, and perfect, will of God"*. (Romans 12:2, KJV) This is why it is important that we who are believers depend upon the word of God that gives us the spiritual perception that we need to recognize deception and how it may affect our lives in Christian living. Deception is sin and those who use such are sinners and have been deceived.

CHAPTER I

WHAT IS DECEPTION SIN OR JUSTIFIED?

People seem to be confused about rather or not it is justified to deceive someone for any reason. People seem to follow their opinions or focus on what they analyze to be the results in the end that justifies their reason. To justify their acceptance of deceiving people they may give reference to the biblical passage in I Samuel 27:8-12 that talks about David's military campaign during his Philistine sojourn. The text actually says nothing about whether deception is right or wrong but is believed to say that God is commending deception. No doubt this thought and understanding has created quite a conserversy among scholars as they search for clarity. One thing for sure deception is a lie and sin however you use it. Many of us have not accepted that fact and chose to challenge the use of it in various parts of our lives giving credit to good intentions. We should know that God hates a liar and a lying tongue. (Proverbs 6:19, 12:22, Col 3:9, KJV)

There are many areas in the Bible where deception has been used but that does not justify its use. God has always dealt with man according to his measure of faith not his intentions or feelings. (Romans 12:3, KJV) David was found to deceive king Achish for several reasons for his own purpose. He persuaded king Achish to believe what was not true about his plan and to take advantage of the opportunity. Some people would consider this idea as great but scripture teaches us that *"there is a way that seemeth right to a man but the end thereof are the ways of death" (Proverbs 14:12, KJV)* David was not acting under God's orders but of his own decision. Basically trying to earn trust from this king in a way that would not satisfy God the true King. We can make all kinds of efforts to deceive someone for the better but the truth is it is still a lie. Giving reference to Rahab the harlot in the Old Testament and her support of the spies that were sent out by Joshua to spy on the land. She deceived the king of Jericho of the whereabout the spies had gone. In other words, she lied to the king knowing she had hid them in her house. She recognized that these were men of God and that God had given them that land and the people were afraid and fearful of the God of Israel. Rahab feared the God of Israel and believed how important it was to help any way she could and hoping to receive a blessing upon the household of her father's house. (Joshua 2, KJV)

Rahab was considered justified by works not by the deception. Her works was based on her faith in God. (James 2:25-26, KJV) The point to be considered is, who gets the glory for what David or Rahab did? David, as the result of his pursuit was not allowed to fight against

Israel and Rahab had allowed an opportunity for the spies to escape that they may continue God's mission to pursue the land that God had given them as well as a blessing upon her father's house. Rahab was of the linage and of the tribe of Judah the same as our Lord and Savior Jesus Christ. To shine a light on the whole controversy of whether or not we should practice deception should point to the word of God that says *" be not deceived, for God is not mocked, for whatsoever a man soweth, that shall he also reap. For he that soweth to his flesh shall of the flesh reap corruption; but he that soweth to the Spirit shall of the Spirit reap life everlasting."* *(Galatian 6:7-8, KJV)* This seems to say that if we practice deception it is because we have been deceived. (Proverbs 14:13, KJV)

CHAPTER II

SELF-DECEPTION

According to Merriam Webster the first known use of the term self-deception was around 1648. Henry Marsh writes, many doctors start to internalize the stories they tell themselves about their superior judgement and skill. But the best, he adds, unlearn their self-deception, and come to accept their fallibility and learn from their mistakes. There is a lot of truth in this statement of what has been expressed. God uses deception not to mislead people but to judge those who have abandoned the truth. Self-deception is clearly the action or practice of allowing oneself to believe that a false or unvalidated feeling, idea or imagination is true. It is a process of rationalizing away the relevance, significance and importance of opposing evidence of logical arguments. Scripture teaches us that if we say we have not sin we deceive ourselves. (I John 1:10, KJV)

An example of self-deception is given in Psalms 36:1-4, KJV that says that "transgression speaks to the wicked deep in heart; there is no fear of God before his eyes. For he flatters himself in his own eyes that his iniquity cannot be found out and hated. The words of his mouth are trouble and deceit; he has ceased to act wisely and do good. He plots trouble while on his bed; he sets himself in a way that is not good; he does not reject evil." (Psalms 36:1-4, KJV) This Psalms has the inscription of David as the servant of Jehovah. It gives us a clear view of the human heart which is wicked. It teaches that every human heart is wicked. (Jeremiah 17:9, KJV) The wicked have an oracle of transgression in his heart that comes from his old nature, the Adamic nature. We can be graceful of how God deals with man's heart. His mercy endures forever and God was revealing the character of the wicked by divine revelation. God's word reveals self-deception in all of us through the Holy Spirit and His word.

Obadiah, a prophet of God, teaches that arrogance is one of the roots of self-deception" *The pride of your heart has deceived you", (Obadiah 1:3, KJV)* human pride will always blind us to the truth. With promises of honor it delivers disgrace. *"Pride goes before distruction, a haughty spirit before a fall" (Proverb 16:18, KJV)* If deception is dangerous then we must consider that self-deception is disastrous. According to Mattew 7:21-23 KJV, *"Not every one that saith unto me Lord, Lord, shall enter into the kingdom of heaven, but he that doeth the will of my Father, who is in heaven. (vs21) "and then will I profess unto them, I never knew you ; depart from me, ye that work iniquity." (vs23)*

Self-exaltation naturally follows self-deception because we deceive ourselves into thinking we are greater than we really are. The father of pride, Satan encourages self-deception that produces pride, after that human nature takes over. A person who exalts himself is he who thinks he stands on his own merits. A sense of well being, power, and importance. It is a self-tribute, self-praise, self-honoring, self-glorifying and self-worshipping. Bible teaches that the fear of the Lord is to hate evil: pride, and arrogance, the evil way, and the perverse mouth, God hates. (Proverbs 8:13)

In conclusion we have learned that none of us can come before God and say that we have accomplished anything of our own strength and hands but know that without God we can do nothing, know nothing, or be nothing without Him. We give praise and honor to God for who he is, the creator of the universe. We have no rights or authority to do anything without God. We have no life and all that is included in it without God. He is worthy of all possible honor, confidence and love as well as worship. So *Let us hear the conclusion of the whole matter: Fear God, and keep His commandments; for this is the whole duty of man. For God shall bring every work into judgement, with every secret thing, whether it be good, or whether it be evil. (Ecclesiastes 12:13-14, KJV)*

CHAPTER III

DECEPTION IN HUMAN NATURE

The fallen human nature of man carries with it a deceitful heart and above all things, desperately wicked. (Jeremiah 17:9, KJV) Since the transgression of Adam in the Garden of Eden against God, all human beings are by nature born sinners. And from within and out of the heart of man comes evil thoughts, adulteries, fornications, murders, theft, covetousness, wickedness, deceit, lasciviousness, an evil eye, blasphemy, pride, and foolishness. (Mark 7:21-22, KJV) By nature this simply defines the fact that the nature of man will never desire to do what is right in the eyes of God. And according to scripture this will result in the reason why everyone must be aware of his neighbor and put not trust in any brother, for every brother is a deceiver, and every neighbor goes about as a slanderer" (Jeremiah 9:45)Jeremiah wept over the spiritual condition of his people and this was why he was called the "weeping prophet." (Jeremiah 9:18, KJV) Even today it is in the nature of man to deceive one another for selfish reasons. "They conceive trouble and give birth to evil," and their womb prepares deceit. (Job 15:35, KJV)

Since deceit is already in the nature of man, how presentable is he to Satan who will take advantage of man for his own purpose? For he is the deceiver of mankind and the father of lies. Only through the word of God can we receive strength and knowledge to overcome this adversary of death. Though we have a fallen nature God has made a way through Jesus to be transformed into a new nature that will instruct us that *we may prove what is that good, and acceptable, and perfect will of*

God ." (Romans 12:2, KJV) In renewing our minds we will grow spiritually in the grace and word of our Lord and Savior Jesus Christ. And though we are children of God, it does not appear what we shall be but we know that when he shall appear, we shall be like him for, we will see him as he is. (I John 3:2, KJV) We will have an everlasting nature that serves and praises God 's purpose throughout the future ages of eternity.

One of the examples and experiences in scripture was stated by Paul *"Oh, wretched man that I am! Who shall deliver me from the body of this death? I thank God through Jesus Christ, our Lord, So, then, with the mind I myself serve the law of God; but with the flesh, the law of sin"* (Romans 7:24-25, KJV) The Spirit delivers from the old nature, producing righteousness.

CHAPTER IV

DECEITFUL HEARTS

You cannot talk about deceitfulness without relating it to the character of a man's heart. It may not have been chosen so but has been the result of the sinful nature of his fall. Our hearts were originally from our creator and was perfect from the beginning. (Genesis 1:26,2:7 KJV) But because of the voluntary transgression of man the nature of his heart became deceitful. In other words disobedient to the will of his creator allowing sin and death to enter the path of his life. A mans heart is his guide and responsibility to manage all his life. *"For as he thinketh in his heart, so is he. Eat and drink, saith he to thee; but his heart is not with thee," (Proverbs 23:7 KJV)* Isaiah states that "

He feedeth on ashes; a deceived heart hath turned him aside, that he cannot deliver his soul, nor say, Is there not a lie in my right hand?" (Isaiah 44:20 KJV) This sinful nature has a profound effect on his life and his relationship with his creator.

"The pride of thine heart hath deceived thee" says the scripture (Obadiah 3 KJV). This was the first sin (pride) coming from Satan himself resulting from him being casted out of heaven to the earth. (Isaiah 14:12-17, KJV) Apparently deceitfulness began with a prideful heart. *(The fear of the Lord is to hate evil, pride, and arrogance, and the evil way, and the perverse mouth, do I hate."(Proverbs 8:13,KJV)* We don't realize it but *"the heart is deceitful above all things, and desparately wicked; who can know it?(Jeremiah 17:9,KJV)* This deceitful heart affects our thinking, our desires, our perceptions even our worship of the creator. There can be no righteousness in itself since it brings about blindness and unfaithfulness. Man cannot heal himself of this deceitful heart. It can only be done by being rooted and grounded in Christ

by faith. (Ephesians 3:17, Philippians 4:7 KJV) And as the result of this, the Lord will direct your heart into the love of God, and into the patient waiting for Christ. (II Thessalonians 3:5,KJV) Living a life of deceitfulness is a life of darkness and lies. This is why the Bible teaches us that we should *"let it be the hidden man of the heart in that which is not corruptible, even the ornament of a meek and quiet spirit which is in the sight of God of great price." (I Peter 3:4,KJV) A deceitful heart defiles a man and effects every part of his life including his worship.* Even though receiving a deceitful heart in our sinful nature does not mean that we don't have a choice to reject that spirit. God has given us precepts and an opportunity to be transformed by the renewing of our minds. (Romans 12:2, KJV)

A man of a deceitful heart, known as a hypocrite, will try to deceive God, but he can't. He can however deceive men most of the time but always himself. The same with profane sinners, the self-righteous and the false teachers, who try to deceive the very elect, but they can't. A good man can be deceived by his own heart like Peter in a sad reference . (Matthew 26:33, KJV) Let us not forget that man is the target of Satanic deception. (Luke 22:31-32,KJV) *"And the Lord said, Simon. Simon, behold, Satan has desired to have you, that he may sift you as wheat; But I have prayed for thee, that thy faith fail not. And when thou art converted, strengthen thy brethren".* Obviously Peter was, as it were, the wheat with his self confidence not realizing that it was his faith that was about to be tested by the Lord. It was the Lord who allowed Satan permission to test Peter teaching him not to rely on deception. A very important lesson was taught here by the Lord to Peter and that is *"if we say that we have no sin, we deceive ourselves, and the truth is not in us. (I John 1:8. KJV)* The recognition of indwelling sin is important in our service to the Lord that we learn how much we need him at all times especially in allowing his Spirit to lead us. It reminds us of the fact that we still possess an old nature, still need forgiveness for our sins and need to know how to walk in the light of fellowship with the Father.

CHAPTER V

THE PRACTICE OF DECEPTION

To shine a light on the subject of deception is to be preceptively aware of our nature and where we stand in our spiritual character. It should not be presumed that it is a natural way of life but a personal choice with reason. The wickedness of a man's nature almost assures him that he will not have complete control in monitoring his choice to deceive. As scripture states *"For as he thinketh in his heart, so is he"*. *(Proverbs 23:7, KJV)* A person who lives a life of deception has no doubt been deceived himself. To practice a life of deception is to practice a life of lies, false hood and unrighteousness.

"The heart is deceitful above all things, and desperately wicked; who can know it? (Jeremiah 17:9, KJV) The Bible teaches that *" He who would love life and see good days, let him refrain his tongue from evil, and his lips from speaking deceit" (I Peter 3:10,KJV)* and *do not be a witness against your neighbor without cause."* (Proverbs 24:28, KJV) *God hates the bloodthirst and deceitful man. (Psalms 5:6, KJV)*

Sometimes we don't realize the deception that is being displayed in our lives. It easily shows in our attitudes, desires and communications. Take for example the stating of a white lie. It's still a lie! to deceive someone. The color doesn't make it acceptable but deceptive of the real thing. We find it easier to deceive than to tell the truth. When we deceive someone else we are only deceiving ourselves. *"Be not deceived for God is not mocked, for whatever a man soweth that shall he also reap"(Galatians 6:7,KJV)* The Bible teaches us that we should *" let no man deceive you. He who practices righteousness is righteous, just as he is righteous."(I John 3:7, KJV)* The sin of deception can be found in all of us on a daily basis because it is in our nature starting with our hearts. This is why we should pray all the time instead of trying to monitor our life without God. Our faith in the Spirit of God and His word will keep us from falling into temptation. It will teach us to trust in His love and lean not on our own understanding but in all our ways acknowledge Him and He will direct our path. (Proverbs 3:5,6,KJV) We need to be reminded that we are the target of deception. Hopefully what starts in the heart will end in the Spirit. This is why we need to have the right perception of God in our lives that we might be aware of His presence at all times. The practice of deception is an abominable thing and God hates it. (Psalms 5:6, KJV) To deceive is to be deceived, this explains the practice of it.

There are common issues experienced in the practices of deception that we may not be aware of. Taking for instance the subject of gambling. A lot of Christians are confused about whether or not gambling is acceptable as long as it is legal. Many don't know what is or is not gambling. Some may even say "life is a gamble" which is a very deceptive way of looking at it. Don't be deceived, life is a sure thing. You are going to live and you are going to die. It is sad to think that there is even a controversy or debate on the issue of gambling. In the scriptures it states that, *"the lot is cast into the lap, but the whole disposing thereof is of the Lord." (Proverbs 16:33, KJV)* This is a clear indication that God is in control of even the results and determination from the gambling. As a matter of fact, throughout the Bible the casting of lots was often used as a method for discovering the divine will of God. (Leviticus 16:8, Numbers 26:55, Acts 1:26,KJV). Men may cast lots to ascertain what the future will bring, but God is still in control. In the Old Testament, God commanded Aaron to cast lots for His purpose as well as Moses. (Leviticus 16::8, Numbers 26:55, KJV) However, in the New Testament, God did not at anytime instruct the casting of lots for future signs. As a matter of fact, God told us what the future holds as much as He wanted us to know. (Hebrews 1:1-2, KJV) That future was based on salvation not riches. You can't win salvation, you can only lose it. (not take advantage of the opportunity)

In the book of Proverb, we will find these words, *"He that hasteneth to be rich hath an evil eye, and considereth not that poverty shall come upon him"(Proverbs* 28:22, KJV) Question is, have you seriously considered why you are gambling? There are all kinds of excuses all deceptive. Some say its only fun, some say its an investment, and some say it is a chance to get rich. Whatever your excuses might be, just remember that God is only interested in the motive behind everything you do. In most cases its deceptive. God knows whats really in your heart even the lack of knowledge. The truth of the matter is that gambling is a trial of chance, a trap of deception or as you put it "luck". We are not questioning the legality but the morality of the practice of gambling. "Luck" implies another form of power that seems to have control over riches, winning or a way out of trouble. It is from the vocabulary of fools. Many people turn to gambling as if it were a God; even after God tells them to pray and ask him and He will give of them. But even Satan's children know that they will get nothing from God, so quite the contrary they don't ask, Luck or gambling presents itself in a persuasive way as to attract and deceive those who believe in luck or gambling to be the solution to their problems. They may even find themselves not being able to love without a continuous desire to hope and believe in the power of luck or gambling as a substitute for God. We call this not only disobedience but "Idolatry". Of all the sins mentioned in the Bible, God hates idolatry the most. He states that *"thou shall have no other Gods before me" (Exodus 20:3. KJV)* Satan is a deceiver and liar. He uses things to attract your perceptions and ideas, And because of your sinful nature, and if you have not the Spirit of God, you will not be able to resist the temptation. Satan's plan is to make you feel in control of your life and your decisions. He will deceive you into thinking there is no harm in gambling especially in considering the possibilities of riches gained. And being able to give an offering to the Church. There is no justification for sin in any form even in good intentions. But Satan will persuade you through temptation that it is justified. But *"Be not deceived for God is not mocked, for whatsoever a man soweth that will he also reap" (Galatians 6:7, KJV)*

People don't realize that moral standards and values are affected by gambling. We are actually learning to trust in ourselves and our abilities rather than in the word of God. God did not institute gambling, man did. And casting of lots should never have been interpreted as gambling. Some how men have been deceived that gambling overcomes God's will just as they think that they shall overcome because of their hope and faith in gambling especially if they win. Gambling is, believe it or not a form of idolatry and stealing. People who gamble are actually worshipping because "worship" means to whom or what you give tribute to. People who gamble do not believe that God is in control of the results of anything in the past, present, and future including the casting of lots. Even though they may say "thank God "for their winning, which God are they referring to? So why should we take gambling so seriously? Because *"there is a way that seemeth right to a man, but the end thereof are the ways of death" (Proverbs 14:12, KJV)* Don't let Satan rob you of your gift, it is a lot to cast.

As I said earlier the casting of lots is not gambling as some have been told. That is a misconception. The difference between casting lots and gambling, if you do a study on it, is in casting lots you don't have to pay to play but in gambling you do.

CHAPTER VI

THE JUDGMENT OF DECEPTION

The judgments of the Lord are clear in scripture pertaining to deception. Even though we are targets of deception because of our nature does not give way to the practice of deception. We have been warned from generation to generation by the word of God to be aware of those who practice deceit. *"Their tongue is like an arrow shot out; it speaketh deceit. One speaketh peaceably to his neighbor with is mouth, but in heart he lieth inwait." (Jeremiah 9:8, KJV)* Deception is a practice that should not be taken lightly in any area of our lives whether intentional or not, God forbids. *"Shall*

I not punish them for these things? saith the Lord, Shall not my soul be avenged on such a nation as this?" (Jeremiah 9:9, KJV) Many times as God's children we act as if we are at any time not in the presence of God. It actually becomes a part of our perception and imagination. And by accepting this reality we develop a lack and weakness of our faith. Forgetting that we *"be not deceived, for God is not mocked, that whatsoever a man soweth that shall he also reap."* (Galatians 6:7, KJV) Judgment always falls on the violation of God's statues, even on His children. So too often do we put the Spirit of the Lord to test and realize that the wages of sin is death. (Roman 6:33, KJV) The Psalmist states that *"Thou hast trodden down all those who err from thy statues; for their deceit is falsehood. (Psalms 119:118, KJV)*

"Awake to righteousness and sin not; for some have not the knowledge of God." (I Corinthians 15:34, KJV) Those of us who have been warned in the word of God know *that "evil men and seducers shall become worse and worse, deceiving and being deceived." But continue thou in the*

things which thou hast learned and hast been assured of, knowing of whom thou hast learned them, and that from a child thou hast known the holy scriptures, which are able to make thee wise unto salvation through faith which is in Christ Jesus." (II Timothy 3:13-15, KJV)

Nevertheless in the New Testament book of Acts, Peter asked Saphira had she sold the land for so much and she lied basically to the Holy Spirit. *"Peter said to her, how is it that ye have agreed together (with her husband) to test the Spirit of the Lord?"* and she died and they carried her body out also. (Acts 5:9-10, KJV) And the scripture *says that great fear came upon the Church, and upon as many as heard these things. (Acts 5:11, KJV)* We should be fearful of the use of deception starting with ourselves. Interesting also to know that the Psalmist quotes *"O God, will bring them down to the pit of destruction; men of bloodshed and deceit will not live out half their days. But I will trust in you." (Psalms 55:23, KJV)* It is no new thing to Christians to now that judgment begins at the house of God. (I Peter 4:17, KJV) *"and if first begin at us, what shall the end be of them that obey not the gospel of God."(I Peter 4:17b, KJV) "For we must all appear before the judgment seat of Christ, that everyone may receive the things done in his body, according to that he hath done, whether it be good or bad. (II Corinthians 5:10, KJV)* That means believers and non-believers. Jesus says, this is the reason he came into the world. (John 5:22, KJV) As we think about the coming judgment and our relationship with the Father we should thank God for His mercy, His presence and His forgiveness for our shortcoming. Even now we have the opportunity to build a relationship with Him and not be ashamed of the Gospel for it is the power of God unto salvation. (Romans 1:16. KJV) It certainly will not just be deception that will be judged but sin in all forms. If we would consider that even though God has known us even before the foundation of the world. He has exercised his love and mercy along our journey through life, giving you the opportunity to know Him and accept His gift of our Lord and Savior Jesus Christ. Who in term has paid for all our sins that you will not have to be condemned but redeemed. And has given you eternal life. You don't have to understand it, just trust God. Its called "faith".

CHAPTER VII

DECEPTION THROUGH FALSE TEACHERS

In scripture there was not only a warning against deception, there was a warning against false prophets and teachers. The warning was to God's chosen people Israel and they were written for their admonition. (I Corinthians 10: 11, KJV) Of course we should give this same reference to not only Israel but to the church today. (I Peter 2:9, KJV) This should not just be a warning but a reminder of what God had spoken *"beware lest thou forget the Lord, who brought thee forth out of the land of Egypt, from the house of bondage." (Deuteronomy 6:12,*

8:11, KJV) This was also a test to see if they loved God with all their heart. Peter draws upon all the apocalyptic passages he knows concerning false teachers that was unacceptable to God who are headed to destruction as his enemies. Peter warns that these false teachers will be in the church and will bring with them false doctrine and the people will not even realize it. Teaching that led to destruction, destroying their faith if they believe. This is the result of them denying the Lord that bought them. (Deuteronomy 6:12, KJV) It also could be that Christ was not their Lord to begin with. (I John 2:19, KJV) Paul mentions in his letters that in the end times there will be a great apostasy. (II Thessalonians2:3, KJV) This was also a concern for Peter and the church knowing that many will follow these teachers. It is clearly understood that these false teachers are in it for the money. (I Peter 5:2, KJV) They are no doubt God's enemies and will be judged.

Concerning the false teachers, Paul informs one of his most reliable helpers as well as the church that " *there are many unruly and vain talkers and deceivers, especially they of the circumcision, whose mouths must be stopped, who subvert whole houses, teaching things which they ought not, for filthy lucre's sake." (Titus 1:10-11, KJV)* Here the need for elders arose in the church because of the false teachers. Even today elders are needed who are sound and firm in the word of God. Even so in the book of Matthew Jesus says to the Pharisees *"ye also outwardly appear righteous unto men, but within ye are full of hypocrisy and iniquity. (Matthew 23:28, KJV)* Some believe that even in this day as we have been warned that the time will come according to Paul to Timothy in his second letter that there will be itching ears being tickled by preachers who don't preach the Bible but to an ungodly congregation who desires to hear what pleases them. Not knowing that they are being turned away from the Gospel of Christ. Paul expounds on the fact that these false teachers know nothing and don't realize that they know nothing. They should be avoided in the house of God and subject to removal.

Knowing what has been revealed to us even by the Spirit of the Lord and His brother Jude, whose message was one of the most severe in the New Testament. He was occasioned by apostasy in the early church because these heresies were so threatening that the Spirit caused Jude to write a letter to the church and readers to earnestly contend for the faith that was delivered by the saints. (vs 3, KJV) He could see how the prevalence of the false teachers had already intruded into the local church and showed vividly how apostasy leads to sinful living. (vs 5- 19,KJV)

Those who are led by the indwelling of the Spirit of God shall realize that the false prophets also claim spiritual leading. But we are warned by John that believers not accept the teachings of these false teachers the things that are contrary to what they have already received from the apostles. In other words, check out the standard principles that never change which is the Word of God. (I John 4:1,KJV) We are reminded that *"false apostles, deceitful workers, transforming themselves into the apostles of Christ, and no marvel for Satan himself is transformed into an angel of light."* Therefore, it is no great thing if his ministers also be transformed as the minister of righteousness, whose end shall be according to their works. (II Corinthians 11:13-15, KJV) The Lord has given us everything we need including His Spirit to recognize false teachers and how to relate to them according to His Word.

CHAPTER VIII

DECEPTION FORBIDDEN BY GOD

Because the truth taught is commanded by the life we live," *we have renounced the hidden things of shame, not walking in craftiness, nor handling the word of God deceitfully, but by manifestation of the truth commending ourselves to every man's conscience in the sight of God."(II Corinthians 4:2, KJV)* A reminder by Paul of our ministry in the Lord Jesus Christ. That we should " *let no man deceive you by any means; for that day shall not come, except there be a great falling away first, and that man of sin be revealed, the son of perdition, who opposeth and exalteth himself above all that is called God, or* *that is worshipped, so that he, as God sitteth in the temple of God, showing himself that he is God. (II Thessalonians 2:3-4, KJV)* God forbids this deception. Peter says "*he that will love life, and see good days, let him refrain his tongue from evil, and his lips that they speak no guile; "let him eschew evil, and do good; let him seek peace, and pursue it." (I Peter 3:10-11, KJV)* likewise says Titus, *"For there are those who profess that they know God, but in works they deny him, being abominable, and disobedient, and unto every good work reprobate." (Titus 1:16, KJV)* God curses and forbids a deceiver who hath in his flock a male and vows it, and even sacrifice it to the Lord that is blemished.* In other words, this was deception demonstrated in the form of their attitude towards their offering and their substitution of offerings. The priest snorted and sniffed as they went about their religious service, treating it with utmost contempt. God forbids and will be feared. (Malachi 1:14, KJV)

One of the deceitful practices that we must be aware of is Idolatry which God hates.

Especially because of the influence that it has on God's people worshipping Him. Not only did God warn His people about *idolatry*, He commanded them to " *take heed to thyself that thou be not snared by following them, after they are destroyed from before thee, and that thou inquire not after their gods, saying,*" *how did these nations serve their gods? even so will I do likewise.*" (Deuteronomy 12:30, KJV) God forbids this deception and says, *"thou shall not do so unto the Lord thy God; for every abomination to the Lord, which he hateth, have they done unto their gods."* (Deuteronomy 12:31, KJV) This still seems the be a major problem today even in the church where believers have stepped outside of the word of God in how they have been taught of how to worship and serve God. They have taken upon themselves to worship God in their own ways and perceptions. They want to interpret God's instructions in ways that pleases their life styles. They have turned away from the truth and had their perceptions blinded because rejection of spiritual truth brings spiritual deception as well as divine consequences. They want to do things the way other churches do when we all are suppose to be members of the same body. Be not deceived! What kind of message would we be sending about our ministry, our teachers and the truth of God's word if we are not on one accord? Spiritual deception is a form of punishment for willful sin and God forbids it. When forbidden techniques are used deception will be the gain, especially in our worship and serving God. All forms of devinate such as occultism, fortune telling, psychic etc. to name a few are forbidden by God. So why does God forbid deception? Because deception is sin and God hates sin.

CHAPTER IX

HOW TO AVOID DECEPTION

Deception is the practice of deceit and no one really desires to be deceived. If we would recall the beginning of mankind, *Adam was not deceived; but the woman, being deceived, was in the transgression." (I Timothy 2:14, KJV) "Notwithstanding, she shall be saved in childbearing, if they continue in faith and love and holiness with sobriety." (I Timothy 2:15, KJV)* As the result of this deception, a sinful nature was inherited in their lives. To be more specific, death entered. Satan did not deceive Adam but he was deceived by his wife Eve who was deceived by Satan. Nevertheless both of them had been deceived. Scripture states that conditionally Eve would be saved in childbearing but a lesson we learn is that the woman is susceptible to be "led away." (II Timothy 3:6, KJV) From this we also learn that *"deception"* is the number one enemy of mankind. And being now a part of our nature hidden in the heart of man, deceit is one of the prime elements of the natural heart. (Jeremiah 17:9, KJV) Notice the condition stated in Paul's letter to Timothy of how "they" would be saved. *"If they continue in faith and love and holiness with sobriety." (I Timothy 2:15, KJV)*

Given the understanding of what has happened to the both of them we realize that we are now in spiritual warfare and should be aware at all times that we need the presence of God and that it is not good for man to be alone. (Genesis 2:18, KJV) Avoiding deception is not going to be easy especially for man alone. In this world we will have trials and tribulations but that does not compare to the spiritual warfare that effects our bodies, souls and spirit. Paul cries, *"Oh wretched man that I am! Who shall deliver me from the body of this death?" (Romans 7:24-25, KJV)* The answer is Jesus Christ our Lord. We understand now that the flesh wars against the Spirit in an on going basis. (Galatians 5:17, KJV) Our enemies are clearly recognized as the flesh, the world and Satan. Deception is a tool used by taking advantage of our nature to challenge temptation and the foundation of life that we stand on. Hopefully the word of God. The only way to practice avoiding deception is to have a relationship with Christ. Know what is expected of you in your relationship with Him. Stay in his word and beware of the presence of the Spirit at all times.

The Bible teaches us to *"be not deceived for God is not mocked for whatsoever a man soweth, that shall he also reap". (Galatians 6:7, KJV)* Rejection of spiritual truth brings in spiritual deception and this can result in spiritual blindness. We should not allow deception to get in the way of our spiritual growth or service to God. Satan would want us to remain in blindness and confusion for his purpose. God is concerned about the effect that deception has on our live especially in our worship of Him. It is important that our perceptions be clear and guided towards all truth that we may be called the children of God. One of the reasons why we cannot make correct decisions about our service to the Lord or righteous decisions is because there is probably a certain amount of deception in our perceptions. We need to always pray and be aware that we are never out of this spiritual warfare. Stay in God's word and give Him praise for his protection, mercy and patience in all that He does because he is a awesome God. Deception is a dangerous and destructive tool of Satan and God hates it. Therefore any man that practices deception it is an abomination to God. (Psalms 5:6, KJV) There are so many ways that we can deceive someone else but it has to start with us. To resist deception it would have to begin with us, our spirit and our relationship with Christ. All of our strength comes from the Lord. Lets take upon ourselves to realize that everything in life has to do with spirituality and that God is in control no matter what. The Bible reminds us that *"We wrestle not against flesh and blood but with principalities, against powers, against the rulers of the darkness of this world, against spiritual wickedness in high places." (Ephesians 6:12, KJV)* Its not just deception that we are avoiding but the sum of it.

Another concern to be aware of is self-exaltation. Self exaltation naturally follows self deception and it is the father of pride. Many spend a lot of time and energy trying to be more than they are. They actually feel that it is necessary to impress others or be above everyone else as their rightful place. Status means more to them in life in order to be successful. They see themselves as earning their respect and friendship from others. This perception only makes them "wannabees" as some would say. God however, is no respecter of persons (Acts 10:34, KJV) This understanding is the result of deception that has been accepted in so many lives. But the Bible says *"though you build high like the eagle, though you set your nest among the stars, from there I will bring you down, declares the Lord. " (Obadiah 1:4, KJV)*

CHAPTER X

DECEPTION: THE POWER OF SATAN

It is not likely that even as Christians do we think about deception as we go about living our lives daily. Our perceptions are usually in obedience and righteous living. But considering the fact that we are aware of the sense of our responsibility to God and our Lord and Savior Jesus Christ, we try not to forget that we are still in spiritual warfare on a daily basis. And from what we are learning in the word of God, Satan, our adversary is still seeking to deceive us and turn us away from God. We have been warned to put on the whole armor of God but never to take it off until death. (Ephesians 6:13-17, Revelation 2:10, KJV) Deception is Satan's most powerful tool and it would seem like there is nothing we can do about it. We are certainly not hopeless as we were promised by God that we do have a choice being God's children that, *"There shall no temptation taken you such as is common to man ; but God Is faithful, who will not permit you to be tempted above that ye are able, but will, with the temptation, also make a way to escape, that ye may be able to bear it." (I Corinthians 10:13, KJV)* Satan has no power except that which God allows. Satan has deceived himself through pride and is an adversary of mankind. He cannot make you do anything only deceive you because of your nature.

"Hast thou considered my servant Job, that there is none like him in all the earth, a perfect and an upright man, one who feareth God, and escheweth evil?" (Job 1:8, KJV) God was not inviting Satan to deceive Job but allowing him to test the faith of Job. (as with Peter, Luke 22:31, KJV) Neither did Satan say to God that he was walking up and down in the earth

" seeking whom he may devour." He would not dare say that before the Lord God. This was after the serpent had been curse. (Genesis 3:14, KJV) We know now that there is nothing about Satan that is righteous but that he hates mankind, Ever since Satan and the angels realized their purpose towards mankind, " *Are they not all ministering spirits, sent forth to minister for them who shall be heirs of salvation?" (Hebrews 1:14, KJV)* Satan became furious of this plan of God and rebelled against God and mankind.

"Woe to the inhabiters of the earth and of the sea for the Devil is come down unto you, having great wrath, because he knoweth that he hath but a short time". (Revelation 12:12, KJV) This is why we should be aware of deceptive practices in our lives that start in the nature of our hearts. This is why scripture teaches us to *"examine ourselves, whether you are in the faith; prove yourselves know ye not yourselves how Jesus Christ is in you, unless you are discredited?" (II Corinthians 13:5, KJV)*

The power of Satan should be of no concern

at all to the children of God. God is power and is still on the throne. *"He has set His glory above the heavens" and hast ordained strength because of thine enemies that thou mightest still the enemy and the avenger." (Palms 8:2-3, KJV)* As powerful as deception is there is no power above that which is God himself. The Psalmist clearly states *"The Lord Is my light and my salvation; whom shall I fear? The Lord is the strength of my life; whom shall I be afraid?" (Palms 27:1, KJV)* Those of us who are under the umbrella of faith have no need to worry about the power of deception or for that matter Satan. We should be concerned about how the so called power or authority is used rather than the power itself, even deception. *"For the Word of God is living, and powerful, and sharper than any two-edged sword, piercing even to the dividing asunder of soul and spirit, and of the joints and marrow, and is a discerner of the thoughts and intents of the heart." (Hebrews 4:12, KJV)* Deception in and of itself is not power but is a lie and the truth is nowhere to be found. It destroys hope, love and faith because there is no life in it, only death. *"Be not deceived for God is not mocked for whatsoever a man soweth that shall he also reap." (Galatians 6:7, KJV)*

CONCLUSION

I have concluded that it is important that we become aware of how deception has affected every area of our lives. Not only are our perceptions affected by it but the inner most part of our being. Our service to God and to mankind must be guided by our hearts. We must reconsider the fact that we are in spiritual warfare and that awareness must be accepted and examined in our lives. We are not asked to understand life as we see it but to accept it as we receive it. Deception is not life but death. *"Let us hear the conclusion of the whole matter: Fear God, and keep his commandments; for this is the whole duty of man." (Ecclesiastes 12;13, KJV)*

BIBLIOGRAPHY OF HELPFUL RESOURCES

Bibles

1. The Nelson Study Bible
   Thomas Nelson Inc 1997, Nashville TN
   HKJV
2. The New Scofield Reference Bible
   C. I. Scofield, D.D., Oxford University
   Press, Inc, 1967
3. The Macarthur Topical Bible
   Thomas Nelson Company, Nashville,
   Tennessee 37214

Resource Tools

1. Webster's II New Riverside University
   Dictionary
2. The KJV Parallel Bible Commentary

SCRIPTURE REFERENCES

Chapter 1

Colossians 2:8
Colossians 2:18-23
John 8:4
Genesis 3:4
I Timothy 4:1-3
Ezekiel 28:14-15
Isaiah 14:13-14
I Peter 5:8
Revelation 12:9, 13:14
Romans 1:8, 25
Proverbs 14:13
Psalms 2:1
Romans 7:18-23
Romans 12:2
I Samuel 27:8-12

Proverbs 6:9, 12:22
Colossians 3:9
Romans 12:3
Proverbs 14:13
Joshua 2
James 2:25-26
Galatians 6:7

Chapter 2

I John 1:10
Psalms 36:1-4
Jeremiah 17:9
Obadiah 1:3
Proverbs 16:18
Matthew 7:21-23
Proverb 8:13

Ecclesiastes 12:13-14

Chapter 3

Mark 7:21-22
Jeremiah 9:45
Jeremiah 9:18
Job 15:35
Romans 12:2
I John 3:2
Romans 7:24-25

Chapter 4

Genesis 1:26, 2:7
Proverbs 23:7
Isaiah 44:20
Obadiah 3
Isaiah 14:12-17
Proverb 8:13
Jeremiah 17:9
Ephesians 3:17
Philippians 4:7
II Thessalonians 3:5
I Peter 3:4
Romans 12:2
Matthew 26:33

Luke 22:31-32
I John 1:8

Chapter 5

Proverbs 23:7
I Peter 3:10
Proverbs 24:28
Psalms 5:6
I John 3:7
Proverbs 3:5, 6
Proverbs 16:33
Leviticus 16:8
Numbers 26:55
Acts 1:26
Hebrew 1:1-2
Proverbs 28:22
Exodus 20:3
Proverbs 14:12
Galatians 6:7

Chapter 6

Jeremiah 9:8
Jeremiah 9:9
Romans 6:33
Psalms 119:118

II Timothy 3:13-15
Acts 5:9-10
Acts 5:11
I Corinthians 15:34
Psalms 55:23
I Peter 4:17
I Peter 4:17b
II Corinthians 5:10
John 5:22
Romans 1:16

Chapter 7

I Corinthians 10:11
I Peter 2:9
Deuteronomy 6:12, 8:11
I John 2:19
II Thessalonians 2:3
I Peter 5:2
Titus 1:10-11
Matthew 23:28
I John 4:1
II Corinthians 11:13-15

Chapter 8

II Corinthians 4:2

II Thessalonians 2:3-4
I Peter 3:10-11
Titus 1:16
Malachi 1:14
Deuteronomy 12:30
Deuteronomy 12:31

Chapter 9

I Timothy 2: 14
I Timothy 2:15
II Timothy 3:6
Genesis 2:18
Romans 7:24-25
Galatians 5:17
Ephesians 6:12
Acts 10:34
Obadiah 1:4

Chapter 10

Ephesians 6:13-17
Revelation 2:10
I Corinthians 10:13
Job 1:8
Luke 22:31
Genesis 3:14

Hebrew 1:14   Psalms 27:1

Revelation 12:12   Hebrew 4:12

II Corinthians 13:5   Galatians 6:7

Psalms 8:23   Ecclesiastes 12:13

The Lord gave The Word; great was the Company of those who published it.

Psalms 68:11

Printed in the United States
by Baker & Taylor Publisher Services